ETHICAL ECONOMICS FROM HISTORY TO THE MODERN WORLD

PADMAJA BHARTI

INDIA • SINGAPORE • MALAYSIA

Notion Press

No.8, 3rd Cross Street,
CIT Colony, Mylapore,
Chennai, Tamil Nadu – 600004

First Published by Notion Press 2021
Copyright © Padmaja Bharti 2021
All Rights Reserved.

ISBN 978-1-63850-850-2

This book has been published with all efforts taken to make the material error-free after the consent of the author. However, the author and the publisher do not assume and hereby disclaim any liability to any party for any loss, damage, or disruption caused by errors or omissions, whether such errors or omissions result from negligence, accident, or any other cause.

While every effort has been made to avoid any mistake or omission, this publication is being sold on the condition and understanding that neither the author nor the publishers or printers would be liable in any manner to any person by reason of any mistake or omission in this publication or for any action taken or omitted to be taken or advice rendered or accepted on the basis of this work. For any defect in printing or binding the publishers will be liable only to replace the defective copy by another copy of this work then available.

Dedicated To, My parents Mr Gopal Das and Mrs Meena Rani Das. Loving the people who were always connected to my life and this is my fortune that they are part of my lovely life.

In the forthcoming future, I respect them all and love to attach with their positive vibes, which will be all connecting to my readers.

Padmaja Bharti

To Readers

Market and Mind are not sellable, **future is for sale, because we all live in futuristic world** (E.g., Share Market, Child Future, Gold Recovery, Green Collar Jobs, Society Welfare, Petroleum, Natural Resources, Competitive Market, etc. All these revolves around the future of making money and for better life). But presently, our **future depends upon duty, rule-based ethics and character-based ethics.**

So, Post COVID-19, India's future will be divided into two parts; Investment which depends upon rule-based ethics, Second, Character-based ethics which comes under brand creation, gold value and market potential.

Introduction

"Economic upgrading in your way…

You are the potential of the country…

You need to push yourself and create the right way…"

Most important "mantra," Money can bring money to save our destiny. So, hold it in shares and securities are the best way to bring it back.

Thinking of Economics

Economic upgrading is to define as we move with the higher value and activities in production, technology, knowledge and skills are the ways to benefit profit-driving participation in global value chain.

Thinking of economics, what are the key words that will strike to our brain:-

1. Money
2. Skills
3. Products
4. Knowledge
5. Venture
6. Production

And all are interlinked in economics cycle.

Economic development relied over the productivity, growth-driven by reallocation of labour from less to more productive activities.

Traditionally, a key role is attributed to the manufacturing sector which is argued to provide abundant opportunities for capital intensification, sales and technological change.

Note: - Reference taken from 'Atharvaveda Samhita.'

Atharvaveda – Economics

The responsibility assigned to Lord Brahma is to supervise the methods of offerings and rectify the errors. It has been stated in "Gopatha Brahmana" at 1,3.2 that – "only a part of offerings is processed by Brahma through the application of mind or mental power.

Aitareya Bra. (5.33) declares that there are two routes for executing offerings – first is Vak (Speech) and other is Mannam (Mind).

Three Vedas (Rig, Yajur and Sama) processes are part of offerings through the speech and the other part is processed by Lord Brahma through Brahmaveda (Ataravaveda) applied through the mind.

Actually, Atharvaveda describes the application of both type of ceremonies viz., peaceful affirmation and the witchcraft (Abhicarika) ceremonies.

A particular importance of such application has been accepted for the King. The kind requires performing the 'Shantika-Paustika' deeds and Tulapurusa Mahadana, etc.,

The priest should be expert in application of Athara hymn and Brahmana.

As Athrva is mainly used for the accomplishments of all worldly acts, it would have perhaps due to this reason, called the First Veda.

The other three Vedas, having their metaphysical blessings and fruits, they come in the second number, while writing the introduction of Atharvaveda composed by him, Acharya Sayana observes in the introduction of this Veda that the three earlier Vedas are for spiritual ends while the fourth and last, Atharvaveda is for both worldly and higher purpose.

Atharvaveda is also addressed as Brahma Veda. Actually, this Veda is determined for the use of Lord Brahma, the chairperson of offerings council (Yajna Samsada).

It has been prescribed that Brahma should be well learned with four Vedas but outstanding knowledge is Atharvaveda is unavoidable for him as Brahma Veda contains all that which is separately found in four Vedas.

On account of the priority of the Brahma karma of Brahma, it is construed as Brahma Veda. Atharvaveda has been addressed as Brahma Veda in Gopatha Brahmana, Chandogya Upanisad, etc.,

The most ancient name of Atharva is Atharvagirasa Veda too This composite word Sams containing the two words i.e., "Atharva" and "Angira," two clans of Rsis. As the sage Atharvan born in the family of Angira had given this Veda in the present form, it is called "Atharvaangirasa Veda."

One more thing to be noted is that the hymns of Atharvan are with the deeds of peace and confirmation and the hymns of Angiras are Abhicarika.

According to Kausika Sutra, there are fourteen topics worth decription in Atharavaveda. These are: - (1) Ceremonies and offerings (2) Paustika deeds (3) Anista-Nivarana and Santi Karma (4) Prosperity (5) Administration (6) Accession to and Accomplishment (7) Education (8) Harmony – Sense of unity (9) Pharmaceutical (10) Witchcraft applications (11) Women welfare (12) Interior decoration (13) Provision for regrets (14) Prediction.

Lets end this intro of economics with a sloka from this oldest Veda:

"Yeh Trishapthaha Pashyanthi Vishwa Rupani Bebrathaha"

"Vachaspathibrala Thesha Thanvo Addh Dadathumeha"

Health Wise Economics & Social Concern

- Social worker should motivate and generate volunteers.
- Next level purification towards health remedies.
- Spending on health care and money added health card should be introduced.
- In virtual platform, core of health care system should be promoted.
- National health survey chart added with Aadhar card.
- Corona Health Policy.
- Consumption of fibre products and health business should be motivated through green economy.
- Health comes under better food and poverty protection; Social sector should hold the healthy manner of living.

Eight Ambitious Flagship Schemes of Indian Government

1. Sarva Siksha Abhiyan – Where all children in the age group of 06-14 years to be enrolled in schools by 2010

2. Mid-Day Meal Scheme – Objective to enhance the malnutrition condition amongst children and to give a boost to the enrolment ratio in schools.

3. Rajiv Gandhi Drinking Water Scheme.

4. Integrated Child Development & Service to boost the child condition.

5. Jawaharlal Nehru National Urban Renewal Mission

6. National Rural Health Mission – This is the most important health mission during this COVID pandemic time to enhance the physical boost to the rural areas.

7. Total Sanitisation Campaign – In rural and urban area in our country for more better health condition.

8. MANREGA program – is already working for the development in this country.

    Poverty is largely concentrated in the states such as Uttar Pradesh, Bihar, Odisha, Madhya Pradesh and West Bengal and they account for over 50% of the total poverty in India.

Planning Commission of India in terms of calorie intake 2400K calories per person per day in rural areas and 2100K calories per person per day in urban areas are must for improving the health condition.

Happy & Healthy Business

In the simplest version of making car can maximise living longer because it is spreading happiness, through car trips, people will feel happiness and it is spreading the business also.

Similarly, in tea business, having a cup of tea can spread the business with happiness.

Flea and Road Side Market

These small things and tiny things will be having the feel good factors, gives and stimulates indirect health factors and definitely can create small budget pocket.

Health Sector Development

Markets which are impulsive for the health sector in this current COVID pandemic time. E.g., Sanitizer Industries, Mask making NGO's, etc

Health From Domestic Factor

Healthy lifestyle in the domestic sector are the new ideas for the COVID times. Across the world, countries in domestic markets like Kitchen stuffs, Toddler products, etc.

Healthy Products For Daily Use

Dairy products like Milk, Butter milk, Curd and Paneer which are good in terms of healthy lifestyle is cooking business towards health. And it is good not only for physical health but also for mental health and definitely these things are easily available all over the world in the market.

Contents

1. Why Ethical Economics? 21
2. Three Levels of Economics 26
3. Completive Economics & Ethics 41
4. Natural Resources 50
5. Agri Growth and Sustainable Development 64
6. Brand Reputation 77
7. Green Collar Jobs 89

CHAPTER – 1

Why Ethical Economics?

Only outcomes matter to ethical decision-making. An action is morally justified if it produces the best outcomes specifically for the companies. Dollar profits measure the best outcome for companies in the short run.

Considering the consequences for the company itself is certainly not wrong, but it is incomplete as an approach to decision making. Applying a simplistic notion of ethical egoism to the corporation probably misses some significant points that most humans would need to consider.

Let us step back to examine a broader scope of ethical inquiry.

Building An Ethical Framework

There are three main ethical frameworks in modern Western thought—briefly, these focus on outcome-based ethics, duty- and rule-based ethics, and character-based ethics. The three approaches are related to each other.

An economic agent takes an action that produces specific outcomes:

1. Economic Agent
2. Action
3. Outcomes.

Using Alternative Ethical Frameworks

We, from the far-sight of the history have identified three ethical frameworks that shed light.

1. Ethical Egoism. The implicit moral framework used corporate ethical egoism: the notion that the right course of action is expected to produce the corporation's best outcomes. One problem with ethical egoism is that it severely limits the scope of analysis to the self, in this case, the producer of a good.

Since one's actions can produce negative consequences for others, many consequentialists would say that efforts should be judged not merely by their effects on oneself but also by their aggregate impacts on society.

2. Economic Welfare Theory. By considering a broader universe that includes consumers and producers, economic welfare theory. The most "efficient" outcome produces the largest net economic welfare for the entire class of both producers and consumers, not merely to one particular company or its shareholders.

If consumers are misled about the car's safety (not informed about the faulty fuel tank), the outcome is inefficient for society. This outcome does not maximize the dollar value created because consumers could not make informed, rational judgments about buying. Hence, their scope of analysis was too narrowly focused on producing an outcome that economists would generally ascribe to as desirable.

3. Utilitarianism. Other ethicists would dispute the notion that human "welfare" can or should be measured by the net economic value produced in markets. The most famous version of consequentialism is classical Utilitarianism, which postulated that it would be possible and desirable to assess the potential outcomes by way of a different metric: that of the net pleasure (or happiness) produced in society.

Each act generates a certain amount of pleasure and a certain amount of pain that varies in intensity and duration. If we add up all the happiness and subtract all the pain, we end up with the net utility produced. The action that makes the most significant net pleasure or utility is called moral.

Hence, classical Utilitarians would agree with economists that the calculation of costs and benefits should measure welfare. Still, these should not be denominated in dollars and cents but psychological pleasures and pains.

Classical Utilitarians would say the decision would give shareholders a minimal increase in happiness. But the few cases of death and burns to customers would create enormous physical and emotional pain for the victims and their families that likely far outweigh any pleasure generated for shareholders.

Duties and Rules

The different arguments against ethical egoism would come from duty-and rule-based ethicists. These viewpoints vary but derive from the notion that one's decisions ought to reflect one's duty (either to a rational process or to rules given by God).

Milton Friedman, the Nobel Prize-winning economist championed the notion that businesses should focus on making profits. Friedman wrote, "Few trends could so thoroughly undermine the very foundations of our free society as the acceptance by corporate officials of a social responsibility other than to make as much money for their stockholders as possible.

Normative and Positive Ethics

Studying how people reach ethical decisions is called Positive Ethics. Proposing a preferred method of moral decision-making is called Normative Ethics.

Normative ethics is the analysis of how we ought to reach judgments about right and wrong—and an adequate theory of normative ethics would likely contain an implicit notion of how people actually can make ethical judgments (positive ethics).

If a normative theory argues we should decide right from wrong using a physically or psychologically impossible procedure, that theory could not be considered viable. Knowing something about human capabilities is likely to play a part in the evaluation of a moral theory.

CHAPTER – 2
Three Levels of Economics

The idea of an ethical economy includes three levels: Micro, Meso, and Macro levels, and it also deals with the philosophical analysis of the ethical foundations of the economy.

The discussion about ethics and economics and the focus on the idea of ethical economy was initiated by the honest German economist Peter Koslowski (1952-2012), who, over many years, worked on the relation between ethics and economics.

In particular, he was interested in the principles of ethical economy, and later, he also applied this discussion to the foundations of the philosophy of management and corporations.

Koslowski wanted to develop a philosophy of ethical economy. In Peter Koslowski's book Principles of Ethical Economic (2008), we find the basis for such an approach to management philosophy. Koslowski argued that ethics and economics must accept one another and unite themselves in a comprehensive rational action theory.

Koslowski was a rising star of business ethics in Germany during the 1980s. In particular, he focused on a purely ethical approach to the problems of economics and business.

His starting point was here the hermeneutic positions of the German historical school based on Wilhelm Dilthey and Schleiermacher (Koslowski 1995). Koslowski was also strongly influenced by Aristotle (Koslowski 1979). Koslowski also opened up the business ethics approach by considering business ethics from religious ethics and Catholic social teaching. But this was not Catholic social ethics; instead, Koslowski, who was a pupil of Spaemann, was an attempt to found business ethics in Catholic religious philosophy.

According to Koslowski's ethical economy that combined hermeneutics with (Catholic) social theory about the conceptualization of market and society, there is a close interaction between culture, ethics, and economics in the definition of the basis for economic markets.

According to the report of Koslowski, economic ethics or ethical economy is a theory of the economy and ethics. As an ethical economy, it unites ethical and economic judgments and constitutes the complement of political economy. Ethical economy and political economy are linked to the macro-economic and economic theory of rational action. But we can also connect the ethical economy (and business ethics) and philosophy of management.

In this sense, the relationship between the ethical economy and the philosophy of leadership and corporation is that the ethical economy proposes analysing the institutional and economic frame of the reflections about management and corporations' philosophy.

Following Koslowski's approach to ethics and economics, we can propose a general definition of a broad approach to management and corporations' philosophy (Koslowski 1988). This approach would focus on issues like the ontology and epistemology of organizations, including business ethics, business ethics, and management. But we can also say that it opens for reflections on business ethics in the framework of hermeneutics and reflective judgment.

In such a hermeneutical perspective, Koslowski's approach to ethics and economics is not only hermeneutic and Aristotelian—as well as inspired by Thomas Aquinas' view on economics–but it also implies a Kantian view on the legitimacy of business ethics. We can say that Immanuel Kant's distinction between theoretical, practical, and aesthetic reason and judgment helps to define the basis for economics and ethics applied to corporations, firms, and organizations.

From this philosophical viewpoint, the ontology of organizations includes questions like: What is the organization? How do we define organizational identity and personhood? What are the foundations of different corporate systems? Likewise, organizations' epistemology includes questions like What frames our knowledge, and what are the categories of our understanding and reason, and the limits of our conceptions of the world? Accordingly, from the framework of the ethical economy, we can argue that management and economics's philosophy deals with issues of the role of ethical responsibility in economics, individualism, and altruism in economic ethics, the part of ethics in economic rationality, the interactions, and tensions between ethics and economics.

Koslowski summarizes this framework for the work on business ethics and philosophy of economics with the following definition of the ethical economy:

Economic ethics or ethical economy is, accordingly, on the one hand, an economic theory of the ethical and of economics and ethical institutions and rules, and, on the other hand, the ethics of the economy. Like the political economy, it has a double meaning. The theory of ethics uses economic instruments of analysis, a theory of ethics oriented towards economics, just as political economy is a political theory that uses economic analysis tools. But ethical economy or economic ethics is also a theory of the ethical presuppositions of the economy's cultural system, a view of the ethical rules and attitudes that presuppose market coordination and the price system to function. The component of the ethical economy, which is more strongly oriented toward application, is called here "economic ethics" (Wirtschaftsethik).

However, the terms "ethical economy" and "economic ethics" merge and the present work also attempts to deal with fundamental and applied questions of ethical economy and economic ethics. The term "ethical economy" (Ethische Ökonomie) goes beyond the research objectives of economic ethics, understood as the economy's ethics, to achieve an integration of ethical theory and economic theory. Ethical economy must be more than merely "economics and ethics".

But oppositely, the ethical economy can also be understood as the economic theory of the ethical or ethics oriented towards economics. Here, we face the economic theory of ethics.

Koslowski argues that economics and economic theory can help clarify ethical dilemmas and maximize economic calculations in ethical decisions. It is important to emphasize that the economic theory of ethics helps to understand the role of self-interest and maximization in ethical dilemmas. Thus, with this definition, we can say that Peter Koslowski opens to analyze business ethics as a practical philosophy of management. This includes the investigation of themes like corporate social responsibility, values-driven leadership, and corporate citizenship in an ethical economy framework. In the perspective of Koslowski's approach, we can argue for a cultural and historical approach to the economy that includes a system of ethical judgment between law, economics, and politics.

In Koslowski's definition, ethics is about the good and human virtues, while economics concern human institutions' design based on self-interest and economic rationality. Both disciplines are based on human action, and both professions work with a concept of rationality. According to Koslowski, a comprehensive theory of economics cannot be based only on self-interest but must include a broader view of the good. However, ethics must also have a real economic dimension, being aware of the rationality of self-interested economic maximization. Accordingly, as a general concept of political economy, the ethical economy unites economic and ethical judgments. It is important to emphasize that this theory benefits from the available instruments of economic theory (microeconomics, macro-economics, economic analysis) while at the same time also using insights from ethical theory to analyze the goodness of norms and institutional arrangements.

According to Koslowski, pure economic theory is a vital instrument for analyzing rational action to ensure the efficient pursuit of objectives and social efficiency. Political economy generalizes this method to be the economic theory of the political and of the economic dimensions of the political and of the cultural and political dimensions of the economy. Concerning Adam Smith's Wealth of Nations, Koslowski argues that there has been a close link between responsible management, political liberty, and political coordination of the economy with the combination of political and economic measures.

Accordingly, the ethical economy can be defined as the economy's ethical presuppositions and economic ethics theory. This is acknowledged by the new institutional economics that states that market actors and economic markets are not independent of social, institutional, and cultural arrangements in society. Political economy examines the social, legal, and institutional foundations of the market economy (price mechanism, market interaction, supply & demand, profits, ownership, contracts, rights, justice). In contrast, the ethical economy investigates the ethical norms and principles of these foundations based on implied ethical understanding (e.g. trust) and ethical standards of justice of the economic system institutions.

But this dialectical relation between ethics and economics must not forget the ethical economy's point of view as a "material or substantive" concept of ethical economy qua normative theory of the relation of ethics and economics in the idea of goods. There is an interaction between economic and aesthetic concepts of values that necessitates a cultural idea of economics, looking at economic institutions' cultural dimensions, management, and political economy.

So Koslowski considers that the ethical economy consists of three fundamental areas of analysis:

1. The theory of the ethical presuppositions of economics;
2. The economic theory of ethics; and
3. The economic and ethical approach of goods and value-qualities of culture.

Together, this can be said to form an ethical economy of human institutions.

Koslowski considers this ethical economy to return to the older practical philosophy, founded by Aristotle, Kant, and Adam Smith. It is the task of an ethical economy to reintegrate this approach into economic thinking. Ethical economy aims to reintegrate ethics in economic theory to situate the abstract concept of "homo economicus" within society's social and cultural sphere. This means that ethics should be abstract philosophical metaethics and concrete ethical reflection about human action in factual social circumstances. Economic ethics in the ethical economy must be practical ethics dealing with concrete life situations of human activity.

Why do we need an ethical economy today? What is the need to focus increasingly on developing this economic ethics, expressed in political economy, business ethics, and administrative ethics?

Koslowski mentions three critical reasons for creating such an ethical economy:

1) Consciousness of the increasing cultural and ecological side effects of our economic actions and need for their ethical accountability,

2) the rediscovery of the human element in technical, economic science and the growing expectation of the responsibility of leaders of the economy, and

3) the need to counteract a wider separation of the spheres of culture and especially the alienation of the economic world and intellectual and material culture.

The first reason is the problem of unintended side-effects of economic action (externalities). Side- effects are consequences for society, nature, and the culture of economic activity. They are both problems and reasons for the need for economic ethics. Human power over nature is increasing. Therefore practical ethical action and responsibility are essential. In his analysis of side-effects, Koslowski refers to thermodynamics and the necessity of economic systems to adapt and cope with their environments. Our power to destroy the world due to our actions' unintended consequences necessitates ethical reflection about economic externalities.

The second reason for the rediscovery of the human person in the social sciences is that there is no scientific and economic reason in economic sciences. There is always a human element. Economics cannot be a purely physical and natural science because it relies on human action and intelligence. Koslowski, therefore, talks about a human turn in economics, a "re-anthropomorphization" or "rehumanization" of economic scientific understanding of economic activity in organizations and institutions. Koslowski argues that "anthropomorphism" is critical in the post-industrial economy because human engagement in work and production is essential for value-creation. In the post-material service and experience economy, "Bringing the mind back in" has become crucial. A re-moralization of the economy is necessary to deal with the cultural influence of the economy, which is expressed by the generalization of the human element in the economy, and we can add because of our move to an "Anthropocene" era of the relation of humanity to nature and the Earth.

The third reason is that it is necessary to have a normative economic activity dimension because the economic element has been generalized to all spheres of society. When the economic system is generalized, it brings the need to deal with the social and ethical aspects of economic activity. Koslowski argues that society's differentiation has led to the generalization of one subsystem, namely the economic subsystem. At the same time, there has been increased separation between the sphere of work and leisure. But the economic and instrumental approach has also started to dominate the sphere of peace. However, this cannot be accomplished without concern for the cultural dimensions of economic action. Therefore, we need to integrate ethics and economics when we deal with the generalization of the economic approach to all spheres of society. A political and ethical economy is necessary because of the extension of economics to all parts of society.

Indeed, Koslowski defines his ethical economy as a postmodern economy moving beyond the modernist economy of Hobbes, Mandeville, and Adam Smith, and also Marx, separating ethics and economic activity. The attempt to make economics a mathematical and mechanical theory, thus separating ethics and economics has failed. The attempts to separate ethics and economics, with personal ethics on the one side and economic rationality on the other side cannot be maintained in Koslowski's perspective of a postmodern ethical economy.

Accordingly, Koslowski was very open to postmodernism since he wanted to be open to new ethics and economics elements (Koslowski 1988). Therefore, it is right to characterize Koslowski's position as an open historical-hermeneutic position of Aristotelian origins in the ethical economy rather than a closed Catholic position, even though there are religious elements Koslowski's point of view.

Jörg Althammer from the University of Ingolstadt follows Peter Koslowski in his development of an ethical economy as a general theory of political economy and an idea of society's economic dimensions, social issues, and family policies (Althammer 2000). Althammer criticizes the instrumental character of the framework conditions proposed in the theory of order ethics. Instead, we can say that the ethical economy searches to define the ethical basis for the economy, as suggested by Koslowski. Ethics cannot be reduced to economics. Instead, it is necessary to determine the right honorable conditions for economic activities about the definition of the good about ethical decision-making in the economy. The ethical approach criticizes the instrumental economic approach as not sufficient for dealing with a good society's ethical conditions. As suggested by Karl Homann based on the US-professor Buchanan, the order ethics approach does not consider these ethical conditions of the economy.

The ethical economy approach is, according to Althammer, also critical to the principles of discourse within the theory of communication ethics. This approach is considered contradictory since the communication dialogue without power is impossible. Moreover, the neutral moral point of view is not possible. It is not possible to define the moral basis of this communicative approach to the ethical economy. Instead, Althammer proposes to base the ethical economy on natural law and Catholic societal ethics. This approach looks at the economy's natural-law foundations as based on individual rights and capabilities (i.e. following Amartya Sen). With this approach, Catholic natural-law thinking tries to define the market economy's limits about the market's economic activity. This approach establishes normative systems of economic order that go beyond the ethics of the market as suggested by the order ethics school of Homann and his colleague Ingo Pies. In contrast to the ethics of the market, with its criticism of the social state and the welfare state, Althammer's and Koslowski's school's approach suggests ethical limits to the economic system based on social and political regulation of the market.

Following Sen and Nussbaum, the capability approach represents such a normative approach to the ethical economy within the welfare state. Concepts of corporate social responsibility, corporate citizenship, and social entrepreneurship find their meaning within the social welfare state's framework concept. The ethical economy is business ethics or managerial ethics. Still, it is instead the intense effort of the ethical economy approach to developing a general normative political economy to regulate the economic market. This economy focuses on the concept of the social welfare state about the regulation of the economic market. The ethical economy's position integrates philosophical reflections about the market's justice and constitutional foundations in the thoughts about the economy's ethics. The ethical economy aims to study the ethics of the market and look at the welfare state's societal institutions and find the right relations between market and state. According to Althammer, this has to be based on a humanism of solidarity in contrast to the market's economic egoism based on "homo economicus". One way to discuss this is the reflections about the minimum conditions of the social welfare state based on social support to individuals, such as minimum basic income.

My question is, now: How can we set up a research program to reinitiate the ethical economy, for economic ethics to be operationalized? What would be the significant tasks of research in the ethical economy today? What is the "research gap" to be initialized for an ethical economy in contemporary research? Is there room for a research project on the ethical economy?

Topics for the analysis in terms of the ethical economy are:

1. The relation between economic ethics and formal philosophical ethics;

2. Definition of the principles of substantive ethics of ethical economy;

3. Ethical economy and cultural philosophy of the economy;

4. Ethical problems and dilemmas about economic externalities and side-effects;

5. Economy, ontology, decision-theory, and philosophy of management, including practical dimensions of decision-making;

6. Economic ethics and the market economy, including specific economic dilemmas of organizations' business ethics and economics;

7. The concept of justice and just price in economics and economic institutions.

We could define this research project with the following issues:

1) Identify the significant dimensions of the ethical economy, based on literature review and analysis of the existing positions and literature in the field.

2) Identify major empirical areas of research in the ethical economy related to economic institutions, political decisions-making, corporate cultures, and organizations

3) Propose solutions for actions and decision-models for economic ethics and ethical economy in different organizations and institution

-x-x-x-x-x-x-x-x-x-x-x-x-x-x-x-x-x-x-x-x-x

CHAPTER – 3

Completive Economics & Ethics

Economists study (capitalism, profits, competition) with concepts that ethicists use (suitable, admirable, best). Ethics studies values and virtues. A deal is good to be achieved or a standard of right to be followed, while integrity is a character trait that enables one to perform the good or act rightly. For example, a list of core goods might include wealth, love, and freedom.

A corresponding list of virtues—or character traits—might consist of:

- Productiveness enables one to achieve wealth.
- Honesty enables one to enjoy loving relationships.
- Self-responsibility enables one to live in freedom.

Ethical issues connect intimately with economic problems. Take the economic practice of doing a cost-benefit analysis. You could spend one hundred dollars for a night on the town, or you could donate that one hundred dollar to the reelection campaign of your favorite politician. Which option is better? The night in the city increases pleasure. A politician's successful campaign may lead to more liberty in the long term. We regularly make decisions like this, weighing our options by measuring their likely costs and likely benefits against each other.

This connects economics directly to a significant ethics issue: By what standard do we determine what counts as a benefit or a cost? A list of competing candidates for the status of the ultimate value standard includes happiness, satisfying God's will, long-term survival, liberty, duty, and equality.

Economists implicitly adopt a value framework when beginning a cost-benefit analysis. Different value commitments can lead to the same item being considered a cost from one perspective and a benefit. For example, those whose standard of value is increasing human happiness would count a new road to a scenic mountain vista as a benefit. In contrast, those whose ideal is maintaining an unchanged natural environment would count it as a cost.

The results of the economic analysis also lead directly to ethical issues. For example, one work of the nineteenth- and twentieth-century debate over capitalism and socialism is a consensus that capitalism effectively produces wealth and socialism effectively keeps people low. Advocates of capitalism use these results to argue that capitalism is good; others might respond that "socialism is good in theory, but unfortunately it is not practical." Implicit in the capitalist position is the view that practical consequences determine goodness. By contrast, implicit in the work of those who believe socialism to be an impractical moral ideal is the view that virtue is distinct from practical consequences.

This connects economics to a second major issue in ethics: Is goodness or badness determined by real-world practical consequences or by some other means, such as revelations from God, faith in authorities or traditional institutions, appeals to rational consistency, felt senses of empathy, or an innate conscience? The point for economic analysis, most of which is a matter of understanding and predicting the consequences of various actions, is that the relevance of economic analysis to policymaking depends, in part, on what one believes is the final source of value standards.

So far, we have two ethics questions that bear directly on economics:

1) What is the standard of good? And

2) How does one establish that something is right?

A third relevant question of ethics is: Who should be the beneficiaries of the good? A common assumption of economic analysis is that individuals are rational and self-interested. The third question focuses on self-interest. Is self-interest moral, amoral, or immoral? Is morality a matter of individuals taking responsibility for their lives and working to achieve happiness? Or is character a matter of individuals accepting responsibility for others and being willing to forgo or sacrifice for them? This is the debate in ethics between egoism and altruism.

Healthy forms of egoism hold that individuals should be self-responsible and ambitious in their pursuit of happiness, treat other individuals as self-responsible trading partners and that those who cannot be self-responsible should be treated through voluntary charity. Healthy forms of altruism argue the opposite, holding that morality is primarily a matter of helping those in need, that charity is more moral than trade, and that the most ethical individuals will be motivated by a spirit of self-sacrifice.

Or consider the debates over rent control and minimum wages. By a large majority, economists agree that such policies are not merely zero-sum, as their advocates intend, but rather negative-sum. In this encyclopedia, Walter Block (see rent control) argues that rent controls cause landlords a loss and cause housing shortages that harm some of the lowest renters the most. Linda Gorman (see minimum wages) argues that minimum wages cause employers a loss and destroy jobs for unskilled laborers. These unintended consequences are well known among economists, but there is little sign that rent controls and minimum wages will be abandoned anytime soon.

Why so? In the case of rent controls, part of the explanation involves the political dynamics of urban areas. Many voters are renters: renters believe that rent control is right for them, and politicians sometimes listen to their constituents.

Another major part of the explanation has to do with a great ethic that says that landlords and employers' self-interest counts for little morally and may be sacrificed to help tenants and employees. The thinking is that landlords and employers are richer, and tenants and employees are lower, and thus rich people should be willing to sacrifice profits to help out the poor if necessary. But if we cannot expect the rich to do the right thing voluntarily, then a great ethic will help justify the government's mandating the sacrifice by law.

The moral difference between egoists and altruists on these economic policy issues is between those who see employers and employees as win-win trading partners and those who see employment as exploitation; and between those who see landlords and tenants as trading value to mutual benefit and those who see poor tenants vulnerable to being taken advantage of by rich landlords.

Generalizing from debates over particular policies to evaluations of economic systems as a whole, Adam Smith's famous statement about self-interest from The Wealth of Nations is directly relevant to our contemporary debates about the morality of capitalism:

It is not from the benevolence of the butcher, the brewer, or the baker that we expect our dinner but from their regard to their interest. We address ourselves, not to their humanity but their self-love, and never talk to them of our necessities but their advantages.

Smith is working out a middle ground between traditional ethical theories that have been altruistic in principle and his new (at the time) economic idea that is optimistic about the power of egoistic individuals in a free market. Smith's position is modern and egoistic in accepting that self-interest is natural and beneficial in making capitalism work well; at the same time, Smith is traditionally altruistic in reserving his highest praise for those who take a disinterested perspective on their interests and are willing to sacrifice their interests.

Bracketing Smith's view on one side is a traditional view of self-interest, one still held by most of capitalism's contemporary opponents: Self-interest is amoral or immoral because it is essentially antisocial is based on self-interest, capitalism must be a system of conflict and zero-sum transactions. And because the good of society as a whole is the standard of value, it follows that self-interest and capitalism must be restrained or sacrificed.

Smith's economic insight is to see that self-interest and capitalism do not generate social conflict. His analysis led him to see that self-interested individual would mostly engage in win-win transactions—that the profit motive, property rights, divisions of labor, competition, and other features of capitalism would lead to individual prosperity and social harmony. But Smith retained the traditional ethical belief that society's good as a whole is the moral standard of value.

Bracketing Smith's view on the other side is the view—held by neo-Aristotelians and Ayn Rand, for example—that self-interest is moral and that what justifies capitalism is its protection and enabling of individuals in the pursuit of their individual lives and happiness. This position agrees essentially with Smith's economic analysis of capitalism as a network of win-win transactions, but not with his primary ethical justification.

Both ethical and economic analysis quickly become complicated, and the three questions noted above provide a starting point for integrating the two fields.

Our contemporary debates over environmental values and policies can help illustrate the complex interplay. Ecological arguments are about two categories of human action: resource use and waste disposal. For example, whether we are running out of trees and whether we should drill for oil in Alaska are issues of resource use; and whether toxic chemicals are poisoning a water supply, and whether greenhouse gases are causing global warming are waste disposal issues. Some problems, such as recycling, are issues of both resource use and waste disposal.

We end with the case of recycling metal drink containers as a working example. Part of the motivation for recycling may be a belief that the world is running out of a natural resource—in this case, aluminum. In part, this belief depends on strictly scientific information: How much aluminum is available from the Earth? How much are we currently using?

As mining and processing techniques improve, what effect will that have on aluminum's available stock? Depending on the scientific data, one might conclude that aluminum is becoming more plentiful or scarcer (see natural resources).

Another part of the recycling issue integrates economic considerations. Recycling can increase the available stock of aluminum and save space in landfills. Still, it also has costs: the costs of making and installing recycling bins for empty cans, the monetary and pollution costs of having recycling trucks travel through neighborhoods and businesses to collect the recyclables, the time cost of putting the cans in the right bins, the cost of reprocessing the cans to extract the raw aluminum, and so on. Whether the benefits of recycling outweigh the costs depends on the results of number crunching by economists.

Another part of the recycling issue turns on general political commitments. Given that using resources well and putting trash in its place are valuable, what social institutions should we rely on to achieve those values? Should recycling be voluntary and a matter of market incentives? Should the government mandate recycle as part of a broader order to manage society's resource use and waste disposal practices? (see the tragedy of the commons and free-market environmentalism).

Governing how we approach the above scientific, economic, and political issues is a set of presuppositions of ethical values. Those who think egoistically see the environment as a set of resources for humans to use for their benefit. Humans use natural resources for various economic and aesthetic purposes, and it is vital to human health that specific standards of cleanliness are maintained. On that assumption, it makes sense to ask scientists to investigate the stock of resources and develop techniques for extracting them. It also makes sense to ask economists to do cost-benefit analyses comparing mining and recycling to determine the most cost-effective methods of producing aluminium. The egoistic goal is to preserve, change, or use the environment in ways that increase human wealth, health, and experiences of beauty.

By contrast, healthy forms of altruism, when applied to environmental issues, dictate different scientific and economic priorities. Altruism concerning the environment requires that humans subordinate or sacrifice their interests to other species' needs or the environment as a whole. Given this perspective, the environment is something to be preserved rather than used by humans. Human self-interested values are a lower priority than other species' well-being or groundment as a whole. Scientifically, asking researchers to determine how much aluminium is available for our use becomes a morally suspect activity. Economic recycling then becomes not a matter of a practice worth doing if the cost-benefit numbers work out for us but rather a duty that humans should accept no matter what the economic consequences to themselves.

-x-x-x-x-x-x-x-x-x-x-x-x-x-x-x-x-x-x-x-x

CHAPTER – 4
Natural Resources

Enviromental Ethics

naturally seems that environmental economics and environmental ethics might provide a locus of convergence between economics and ethics. Indeed, a focus on the environment would encourage common perceptions and worldviews. I would argue that just the opposite is more nearly correct.

Environmental economics has carved out a niche within economics by pushing at the boundaries of anthropocentric economic utilitarianism, for example, by incorporating environmental values into the benefit-cost accounts and by extending market logic and market institutions as deeply as possible into the environmental domain. Environmental ethicists have distinguished themselves within the moral philosophy community by concentrating their attack on anthropocentrism, advancing the logic of non-anthropocentric ethics, and developing moral claims on behalf of wilderness and natural processes. The perceived need for validation by the respective mother disciplines – which might be attained via a delicate balancing act of doing creative but methodologically acceptable work within the unique niches they have developed – has led economists and ethicists to pursue their shared environmental focus in quite different directions, thereby undermining any instincts to seek more common ground.

Economy and Society and the Economic Ethics of the World Religions

In the last decade of Weber's life he produced a primary methodological text; 'The Categories of an Interpretative Sociology,' a major systematic work, the incomplete *Economy and Society*, and the bulk of his mature substantive work, 'Economic Ethics of the World Religions.' The essays that make up this work are overly concerned with why a rational capitalism based on calculability originated exclusively in the West. But their larger theme is the general problem of the West's cultural specificity, that is to say the peculiarity, in world terms, of Western political, economic, and legal institutions. But the uniqueness of the West requires an unusual explanation.

The general development of religious ideas corresponds to particular social strata's development, with peasants having a strong affinity for magic, aristocratic classes for a kind of self-justifying, charismatic self-conception. These affinities tend to be relatively stable and do not transform the social structures in which they arise. Consequently, the problem of explanation is to identify the point of openness in which a very specific kind of innovation, namely those that have transformative effects on individuals or groups, might arise. The general promise of religion is health, wealth, and happiness. And the elemental affinities to strata express these needs in forms specific to the strata.

The exceptional cases are the salvation religions, which offer rebirth or redemption, and more generally religions that are doctrinally open to rationalization, producing potentially transformative innovations through rationalization. However, religious rationalization, while producing new coherence or consistency in religious doctrines, characteristically serves to produce discrepancies with other 'spheres' from which religious life is differentiating under the same pressure of circumstance. A general problem which all salvation religions must face up to is the problem of the relationship between destiny and merit, the problem of theodicy, which these religions develop in extraordinarily elaborate ways—ways which on the one hand 'rationalize' the discrepancies by making the fact of evil or bad luck intelligibly consistent with the religious ideology, but also in ways that are consequential for practice. The Chinese solution, for example, was to reconcile the two by recourse to widespread magical tradition, which in turn had negative consequences: a 'deep repugnance to undertaking any change in the established conduct of life because supernatural evils are feared' (1961). Ancient Judaism, in contrast, devised solutions that excluded and repudiated magic, and this carried over into Christianity and consequently into the western worldview in a way that favoured the eventual development of science and technology.

Weber pointed to many similar indirect effects of general institutional conditions, conditions that do not directly determine possibilities but greatly reduce the probability of developments in a particular direction. Rationalization, for example, means the attainment of greater consistency and completeness. Still, the two take various forms for intellectuals and practical persons, such as merchants, and many detailed contingencies govern the direction that rationalization takes in a given situation or in the face of given problems. Weber saw the various forms and processes of rationalization as interacting with one another, that is to say, saw rationalization in one sphere as creating difficulties that require rationalization to relate to spheres, thus producing a dynamic, ongoing process of mutually reinforcing rationalization.

Occasionally Weber appears to slip into the error of regarding the rationalization process as itself a historical force. Still, these rare cases ordinarily can be interpreted in causal, and typically 'interest' terms. For example, the rationalization of modern law on the continent is interpreted as driven by the status interests of law professors.

Investigation of the relation between religion and economic life has long been a central concern of sociological reflection. Still, this topic has been largely defined through debates on the relationship of faith and capitalism, the latter being the specific and dominant expression of economic life in modernity. The work of Karl Marx on the origins and world-historic significance of capitalism, and of Max Weber on the Protestant ethic and the spirit of capitalism' and the economic ethics of the world religions, inevitably overshadow the discussion of both the history and the contemporary forms of the ambiguous and changing relationship between religion and economic life.

However, these classical discussions do not exhaust the topic, which can be represented in the following broad terms. Precapitalist configurations of religion and economic life are often subordinated to the sociological, or socioeconomic, study of Western history, and the anthropological study of primarily non-Western cultures affords vital insights. The emergence of modern capitalism is intimately related to political economy, Marx and Marxism, and to Weber's account of the elective affinities between religion and economic life. Christian religious responses to nineteenth and twentieth century capitalism have been dominated by Roman Catholic social teaching. Now unfettered by ideological confrontation with socialism, contemporary capitalism is best understood as the driving force informing globalization, commodification, and managerialism. It possesses such comprehensive power to provoke and sustain a wide range of contrasting religious responses. Possible futures and research options are focused around the capacity of economic life to destroy and recreate 'nature,' to re-forge the parameters of human self-understanding, and to virtualize humankind's condition. Economic life would seem increasingly to have become 'life' itself.

Weber was an influential comparative historian, legal scholar, economic historian, sociologist, historian of religion, and social scientist. Most of his professional life he was a private scholar in Heidelberg, although for short spells, he lectured at various German universities. He was active in several German scholarly and policy associations, and he coedited the *Archiv fur Sozialwissenschaft,* where he also published many of his essays.

Weber took on the big questions and themes in the social and historical sciences of the late 19th century. The biggest problem was the origins of capitalism in early modern Europe and, more broadly, the specific causes and trajectory of Western rationalism that enabled the West to exit from tradition into modernity and to dominate non-Western civilizations. Though he remained indebted to Marx in many ways, he challenged the dominant Marxian historical materialism. He argued for the unintended but consequential consequences of religion for other, including economic, institutions. Using the comparative historical method and relying on the specialized historical scholarship of his time, he also wrote specific essays and monographs on the evolution of the city as a distinct institution, the decline of the social and economic system of the Roman–Mediterranean world, the Puritan religion's impact on the saints' worldly activities (which he termed "inner worldly asceticism"), the economic ethic of world religions, political sociology, social stratification, nationalism, the Russian revolution of 1905, the stock market, socialism, the sociology of music, and other topics.

Second in importance was Weber's effort to create the foundations for a single social science and counteract the differentiation of the social and historical sciences into specialized and splintered disciplines. In *Wirtschaft und Gesellschaft* he anchored that venture on a theory of action whose primitive elements describing individual human actions are combined and elaborated into aggregate level and relational concepts such as authority, legitimacy, state, and bureaucracy, using the principles of methodological individualism.

Third, he wrote several methodological essays on concept formation; explanation in the human sciences, theoretical concepts and models, the relation of unique events and individual actions to general reasons; the fundamental chasm between fact and value and between science and politics; the role of physical, biological, and hereditary factors in explanations of human behaviour and institutions; the impact of great men on social change; the problem of intersubjectivity in understanding and interpreting human actions; causation in human affairs, and other topics in the philosophy of social science and the logic of social inquiry.

The fourth and the least known, indeed sometimes ignored, part of Weber intellectual output was his empirical studies dealing with social policy issues such as the condition of farm workers in East Prussia and the condition of life and productivity of industrial workers, together with methodological guidelines on how to design and conduct such empirical research. German social scientists in the Verein fur Sozialpolitik concluded that the facts and figures churned out by statistical agencies, which had stimulated the field of "moral statistics," based as they were on official documents such as birth and death registration, crime and suicide records, trade and production figures, public health records, and the like, were not always suited to answering questions scholars and policy analysts were interested in. They organized social surveys for obtaining additional data. Weber was an active participant in a significant 1891–1892 Verein social survey on agricultural labor in East Prussia and a follow-up survey in 1893 by the Evangelical Social Congress. He was the principal intellectual inspiration behind the Verein's 1909–1911 survey of industrial workers, which failed because of a trade union boycott. In preparation of the survey, in the summer of 1908, Weber undertook his most intense empirical study at the textile factory of a relative where he had complete access to personnel, production, and earnings records and the workers themselves in the plant as a participant observer. At the founding of the German Sociological Society in 1910, which Weber conceived as an association for coordinating collective research projects, he outlined plans for a sociology of the press using content analysis and an empirical investigation of voluntary associations "from the bowling club ... to the political party and to the religious, artistic and literary sect." However, these plans were not implemented.

Weber's commitment to empirical social research ran deep. He laboured to teach himself Russian just to read the Russian press on the revolution of 1905. He spent hours doing statistical calculations on factory workers' production records and told university students in his well-known "Science as a Vocation" lecture that "No sociologist ... should think himself too good, even in his old age, to make tens of thousands of quite trivial computations ... perhaps months at a time. One cannot with impunity try to transfer this task entirely to mechanical assistants if one wishes to figure out something ..." He declined to join the Heidelberg Academy of Sciences in 1909 because he believed its resources would be better spent on a social science research institute for undertaking social surveys and postdoctoral fieldwork.

Enterpreneurship

1. The Classical Theories: - The classical interpretations of entrepreneurship by Marx, Weber, and Schumpeter are framed into broad, ambitious studies of economic dynamics and cultural change which, although sometimes not convincing and in need of empirical verification and substantial revision, generally avoid the pitfalls of comparative static models and often ask the right kind of questions.

Marx's contribution to the study of entrepreneurship does not lie so much in *Das Kapital's* (1867) abstract model of the capitalist mode of production, as in the analysis of the capitalist labour market and factory system, and in the historical sketch on 'primitive accumulation,' where he traces the processes of disenfranchising of labour from feudal and corporate ties and the transformation of land, merchant, and money capital into industrial capital; as well as in the accounts of the events of 1848 and 1870 in France, where the different strategies of the various components of the bourgeoisie, such as industrial and financial capital, are analysed.

On the whole, in spite of its methodological errors—first of all the reifying of its economic model into more or less universal laws—Marx's analysis of the rise and the internal dynamics of capitalism played an essential role in future works by Weber, Sombart, Schumpeter, and many others (both Marxists like Dobb, Sweezy, the 'dependencia' theorists, and non-Marxists like Polanyi and Barrington Moore), by identifying a set of necessary structural conditions of a capitalist economy, where entrepreneurship can develop.

Weber's study of entrepreneurship couched in his analysis of the interplay between religious ethos and modern rationalization in the rise of capitalism. The entrepreneur is clearly distinguished from his historical predecessors in traditional economies by his rational and systematic pursuit of economic gain, reliance on calculation measured concerning this economic criterion, the extension of trust through credit, and the subordination of consumption in the interest of accumulation. These are the elements of the rational economic actors 'instrumental rationality' (*Zweckrationalitat*). He or she establishes a systematic relationship between preferred goals and the most suitable means to achieve them. In his ponderous essays on the economic ethics of great world religions published in the *Archiv für Sozialwissenschaft und Sozialpolitik* and in his major work *Wirtschaft und Gesellschaft* on the relations between economy and society, Weber argued that the advent of ascetic Protestantism provided an especially fruitful breeding ground for the mentality of economic rationality since through a complicated process material success is a sign of ascetic realization.

Weber's analysis has been variously and sometimes convincingly criticized. Still, his most significant and lasting contribution lies, as Brigitte Berger (1991) puts it, in his ability to show how the expansion of "instrumental rationality" characteristic of the modern entrepreneurial phenomenon also impelled—slowly and incrementally, through the efforts of individuals and groups in their everyday activities and practices—the formation of distinctly modern institutions in all spheres of life, the public as well as the private.' The degree to which the forces of rationalization responsible for dislodging individuals from their embeddedness in nature, religion, and tradition continue to shape contemporary and future developments in the study of some current researchers, particularly those influenced by Kellner.

The classical interpretations of Marx and Weber are relevant, but Schumpeter is the theorist of entrepreneurship' par excellence,' who provides the most thorough analysis of the entrepreneurial function. The study of entrepreneurship is at the centre of Schumpeter's theoretical system. The entrepreneurial process is the critical variable in his theory of development. He defined it as innovation, introducing a new combination of the factors of production (land and labour) that, when combined with credit, breaks into the static equilibrium of the circular flow of economic life and raises it to a new level. The entrepreneur changes the supply conditions, combines existing resources in new ways, and thereby sets up a new production function. Entrepreneurship does not imply property requisite, is not based on the assumption of risk, and does not require belonging to a business organization. Schumpeter stressed the entrepreneur's revolutionary character (and sometimes portrayed him with the same unilateral admiration as Marx showed for the revolutionary proletariat).

Schumpeter drew on a range of sociological and psychological insights to demonstrate the entrepreneur's unique role and qualities.

Entrepreneurship, he argues, calls for a specific type of personality and conduct, which differs from the economic man. The entrepreneur takes advantage of rationally based components of his or her environment, such as money, science, and individual freedom. He or she orients his or her conduct to rational values. Still, he or she is not the average product of bourgeois culture, which defines rationality from the narrower viewpoint of calculating one's short-term advantage. The entrepreneur acts on the basis of an autonomous drive to conquest and struggle, achieve and create for its own sake, and establish a family dynasty. He or she is a bold leader, capable of thinking the new and grasping the essential, willing to act quickly, to understand by intuition, and to forgo the psychological resistances and social criticisms that always arise when new and innovative behaviour is regarded as deviant and dangerous. This sets him off from the routine manager. While having some elements in common with religious and military leaders of the past, the entrepreneur is, however, the leader of rational and antiheroic culture, and as a result, does not excite the charismatic feelings and collective enthusiasm of those who make or defend whole civilizations.

Entrepreneurship is a specific historical phenomenon, which rests on the premise of a separate economic sphere differentiated from others. In previous epochs, the entrepreneurial function was fused with others in the actions of religious, political, and social leaders. In any historical society, there is leadership, defined as the capacity to conceive and lead innovations. What changes in the different historical contexts is the privileged sphere where leadership is applied, which is related to the core function for the survival and development of that given society. Entrepreneurship is the specific historical form that leadership assumes in capitalism, its distinctive (and even essential) feature, closely linked to the bourgeois class. The bourgeoisie is the top class because bourgeois families have performed the innovating and leadership role in the economy and acquire, consolidate, and transfer prestige, power, and wealth to future generations.

The conception of entrepreneurial innovation as the key element of capitalism implies that the weakening of the innovative entrepreneur's role is seen as a primary factor—along with the fading away of bourgeois institutions—of capitalism's crisis. It is the very success of the capitalist firm that undermines the system.

Schumpeter's identification of the fate of the nineteenth-century entrepreneur with capitalism is mainly responsible for his faulty prediction of this system's collapse. In reality, capitalism has proved capable of fundamental transformations through that process of 'creative destruction' that Schumpeter had perceived but underestimated. Several different brands of capitalism exist, which proved compatible with substantial firms' existence and state intervention and control of the economy.

Despite his limitations, Schumpeter is the most influential scholar of entrepreneurship. Although often in a somewhat sketchy way, he asked the most relevant questions and provided important theoretical insights.

-x-x-x-x-x-x-x-x-x-x-x-x-x-x-x-x-x-x-x-x-x

CHAPTER – 5

Agri Growth and Sustainable Development

The goal of sustainable agriculture is to meet society's food and textile needs in the present without compromising future generations' ability to meet their own needs.

Practitioners of sustainable agriculture seek to integrate three main objectives into their work: a healthy environment, economic profitability, and social and economic equity. Every person involved in the food system—growers, food processors, distributors, retailers, consumers, and waste managers—can play a role in ensuring a sustainable agricultural system.

There are many practices commonly used by people working in sustainable agriculture and sustainable food systems. Growers may use methods to promote soil health, minimize water use, and lower pollution levels on the farm. Consumers and retailers concerned with sustainability can look for "values-based" foods that are grown using methods promoting farmworker well-being, environmentally friendly, or strengthening the local economy. And researchers in sustainable agriculture often cross-disciplinary lines with their work: combining biology, economics, engineering, chemistry, community development, and many others. However, sustainable agriculture is more than a collection of practices. It is also the negotiation process: a push. It pulls between the sometimes-competing interests of an individual farmer or people in a community as they work to solve complex problems about how we grow our food and fibre.

Topics in Sustainable Agriculture

Addressing Food Insecurity

- Agritourism
- Agroforestry
- Biofuels
- Conservation Tillage
- Controlled Environment Agriculture (CEA)
- Cooperatives
- Cover Crops
- Dairy Waste Management
- Direct Marketing
- Energy Efficiency & Conservation
- Food and Agricultural Employment
- Food Labelling/Certifications
- Food Waste Management

- Genetically Modified Crops
- Global Sustainable Sourcing of Commodities
- Institutional Sustainable Food Procurement
- Biologically Integrated Farming Systems
- Integrated Pest Management (IPM)
- Nutrition & Food Systems Education
- Organic Farming
- Precision Agriculture (SSM)
- Soil Nutrient Management
- Sustainable Postharvest Management Practices
- Technological Innovation in Agriculture
- Urban Agriculture
- Value-Based Supply Chains
- Water Use Efficiency
- Water Quality Management
- Zero-Emissions Freight Transport

Directory of Uc Programs In Sustainable Agriculture

The UC Programs | Sustainable Agriculture and Food Systems directory is a catalogue of UC's programmatic activities in sustainable agriculture and food systems. The guide can be searched and sorted by activities and topic areas.

The Philosophy & Practices of Sustainable Agriculture

The rest of this page delves further into the philosophy and practices underpinning sustainable agriculture. Or visit the links to the right to see practical pages for practicing sustainable agriculture.

A variety of philosophies, policies, and practices have contributed to these goals. People in many different capacities, from farmers to consumers, have shared this vision and contributed to it.

Despite the diversity of people and perspectives, the following themes commonly weave through definitions of sustainable agriculture:

Sustainability rests on the principle that we must meet the present's needs without compromising the ability of future generations to meet their own needs.

Therefore, stewardship of both natural and human resources is of prime importance. Stewardship of human resources includes consideration of social responsibilities such as working and living conditions of laborers, rural communities' needs, and consumer health and safety both in the present and the future. Stewardship of land and natural resources involves maintaining or enhancing this vital resource base for the long term.

A systems perspective is essential to understanding sustainability.

The system is envisioned in its broadest sense, from the individual farm to the local ecosystem and communities affected by this farming system both locally and globally. An emphasis on the system allows a more extensive and more detailed view of the consequences of farming practices on human communities and the environment. A systems approach gives us the tools to explore the interconnections between farming and other aspects of our environment.

Everyone plays a role in creating a sustainable food system.

A systems approach also implies interdisciplinary efforts in research and education. This requires researchers' input from various disciplines and farmers, farmworkers, consumers, policymakers, and others.

Making the transition to sustainable agriculture is a process.

For farmers, the transition to sustainable agriculture typically requires a series of small, realistic steps. Family economics and personal goals influence how fast or how far participants can go in the transition. It is essential to realize that each small decision can make a difference and contribute to advancing the entire system further on the "sustainable agriculture continuum." The key to moving forward is the will to take the next step.

Finally, it is essential to point out that reaching toward sustainable agriculture is the responsibility of all participants in the system, including farmers, laborers, policymakers, researchers, retailers, and consumers. Each group has its part to play, its unique contribution to strengthening the sustainable agriculture community.

The remainder of this page considers specific strategies for realizing these broad themes or goals. The designs are grouped according to three separate though related areas of concern: Farming and Natural Resources, Plant and Animal Production Practices, and the Economic, Social and Political Context. They represent a range of potential ideas for individuals committed to interpreting sustainable agriculture's vision within their circumstances.

It has integrated both crop and livestock operations. Indeed, the two were highly complementary both biologically and economically. The current picture has changed quite drastically since then. Crop and animal producers are still dependent on one another to some degree. Even the integration now most commonly occurs at a higher level--*between* farmers, through intermediaries, rather than *within* the farm itself. This is the result of a trend toward the separation and specialization of crop and animal production systems. Despite this trend, there are still many farmers, particularly in the Midwest and North-eastern U.S., that integrate crop and animal systems--either on dairy farms or with range cattle, sheep, or hog operations.

Even with the growing specialization of livestock and crop producers, many of the crop production section principles apply to both groups. The actual management practices will, of course, be quite different. Some of the specific points that livestock producers need to address are listed below.

Management Planning

Including livestock in the farming system increases the complexity of biological and economic relationships. The mobility of the stock, daily feeding, health concerns, breeding operations, seasonal feed and forage sources, and complex marketing are sources of this complexity. Therefore, a successful ranch plan should include enterprise calendars of operations, stock flows, forage flows, labour needs, herd production records, and land use plans to give the manager control and a means of monitoring progress toward goals.

Animal Selection

The animal enterprise must be appropriate for the farm or ranch resources. Farm capabilities and constraints such as feed and forage sources, landscape, climate, and skill of the manager must be considered in selecting which animals to produce. For example, ruminant animals can be raised on various feed sources, including range and pasture, cultivated forage, cover crops, shrubs, weeds, and crop residues. There is a wide range of breeds available in each significant ruminant species, i.e., cattle, sheep, and goats. In general, hardier breeds have lower growth and milk production potential and are better adapted to less favourable environments with sparse or highly seasonal forage growth.

Animal Nutrition

Feed costs are the enormous single variable cost in any livestock operation. While most of the feed may come from other enterprises on the ranch, some purchased feed is usually imported from the farm. Feed costs can be kept to a minimum by monitoring animal condition and performance and understanding seasonal variations in feed and forage quality on the farm. Determining the optimal use of farm-generated by-products is a fundamental challenge of diversified farming.

Reproduction

The use of quality germplasm to improve herd performance is another key to sustainability. Combining good genetic stock, adapting the reproduction season to fit the climate and sources of feed and forage reduces health problems and feed costs.

Herd Health

Animal health greatly influences reproductive success and weight gains, two critical aspects of successful livestock production. Unhealthy stock waste feeds and requires additional labour. A herd health program is vital to sustainable livestock production.

Grazing Management

Most adverse environmental impacts associated with grazing can be prevented or mitigated with proper grazing management:

1. The stock per unit area (stocking rate) must be correct for the landscape and the forage sources. There will need to be compromises between the convenience of tilling large, unfenced fields and livestock operations' fencing needs. The use of modern, temporary fencing may provide one practical solution to this dilemma.

2. The long-term carrying capacity and the stocking rate must take into account short and long-term droughts. Especially in Mediterranean climates such as California, adequately managed grazing significantly reduces fire hazards by reducing fuel build-up in grasslands and brushlands.

3. The manager must achieve sufficient control to reduce overuse in some areas while other areas go unused.

4. The prolonged concentration of stock that results in permanent loss of vegetative cover on uplands or in riparian zones should be avoided. However, small-scale loss of vegetative cover around water or feed troughs may be tolerated if the surrounding vegetative cover is adequate.

Confined Livestock Production

Animal health and waste management are critical issues in confined livestock operations. Today's moral and ethical debate regarding animal welfare is particularly intense for captive livestock production systems. The issues raised in this debate need to be addressed.

Confinement livestock production is increasingly a source of surface and groundwater pollutants, mainly where large numbers of animals per unit area. Expensive waste management facilities are now a necessary cost of confined production systems. Waste is a problem of almost all operations and must be managed concerning both the environment and the quality of life in nearby communities. Livestock production systems that disperse stock in pastures, so the wastes are not concentrated and do not overwhelm natural nutrient cycling processes, have become a subject of renewed interest.

Degrades the natural resource base, the ability of future generations to produce and flourish decreases. The decline of ancient civilizations in Mesopotamia, the Mediterranean region, Pre-Columbian southwest U.S., and Central America is believed to have been strongly influenced by natural resource degradation from non-sustainable farming and forestry practices.

Water is the principal resource that has helped agriculture and society to prosper, and it has been a major limiting factor when mismanaged.

Water Supply and Use.

In California, extensive water storage and transfer system has been established, which has allowed crop production to expand to very arid regions. In drought years, limited surface water supplies have prompted an overdraft of groundwater and consequent intrusion of saltwater or permanent collapse of aquifers. Periodic droughts, some lasting up to 50 years, have occurred in California.

Several steps should be taken to develop drought-resistant farming systems even in "normal" years, including both policy and management actions:

1) improving water conservation and storage measures,
2) providing incentives for selection of drought-tolerant crop species,
3) using reduced-volume irrigation systems,
4) managing crops to reduce water loss, or
5) not planting at all.

Water Quality

The most critical water quality issues involve salinization and contamination of ground and surface waters by pesticides, nitrates, and selenium. Salinity has become a problem wherever the water of even relatively low salt content is used on shallow soils in arid regions and where the water table is near the root zone of crops. Tile drainage can remove the water and salts, but the salts and other contaminants' disposal may negatively affect the environment depending upon where they are deposited. Temporary solutions include the use of salt-tolerant crops, low-volume irrigation, and various management techniques to minimize the effects of salts on crops.

In the long-term, some farmland may need to be removed from production or converted to other uses. Other uses include the conversion of row cropland to the production of drought-tolerant forages, the restoration of wildlife habitat, or agroforestry to minimize the impacts of salinity and high-water tables. Pesticide and nitrate contamination of water can be reduced using many of the practices discussed later in the Plant Production Practices and Animal Production Practices Sections *Wildlife*.

Another way in which agriculture affects water resources is through the destruction of riparian habitats within watersheds.

The conversion of wild habitat to agricultural land reduces fish and wildlife through erosion and sedimentation, the effects of pesticides, removal of riparian plants, and the diversion of water. The plant diversity in and around both riparian and agricultural areas should be maintained to support various wildlife. This diversity will enhance natural ecosystems and could aid in agricultural pest management.

Modern agriculture is heavily dependent on non-renewable energy sources, especially petroleum. The continued use of these energy sources cannot be sustained indefinitely, yet to abruptly abandon our reliance on them would be economically catastrophic. However, a sudden cut-off in energy supply would be equally disruptive. In sustainable agricultural systems, there is reduced reliance on non-renewable energy sources and a substitution of renewable sources or labour to the economically feasible extent.

Many agricultural activities affect air quality. These include smoke from agricultural burning; dust from tillage, traffic, and harvest; pesticide drift from spraying; and nitrous oxide emissions from nitrogen fertilizer.

- incorporating crop residue into the soil
- using appropriate levels of tillage
- and planting windbreaks, cover crops or strips of native perennial grasses to reduce dust.

Soil erosion continues to be a severe threat to our continued ability to produce adequate food. Numerous practices have been developed to keep soil in place, which includes:

- reducing or eliminating tillage
- managing irrigation to reduce runoff
- and keeping the soil covered with plants or mulch.

-x-x-x-x-x-x-x-x-x-x-x-x-x-x-x-x-x-x-x-x

CHAPTER – 6

Brand Reputation

"In a way, this book deals with the other side' of the ethical economy. Using the brand as a paradigmatic example shows how the logic of informational capitalism is about appropriating and extracting value from social communication. Value is no longer primarily based on command over material production but on controlling immaterial production: producing a shared social world through communication and interaction.

The Italian economist Maurizio Lazzarato calls this the output of an 'ethical surplus'- a term I like. He also says that the characteristic thing about informational capital is that 'surplus value becomes premised on the ability to extract an ethical surplus.' The brand is the perfect mechanism to achieve just that.

If you think of it, a brand is a strange kind of object. It is not merely a symbol of a product (that was true up until the 1950s, more or less), nor is it only an extension of a product, an immaterial extra as in Camel cigarettes or the life-style of Camel cigarettes the ethical engagement of

Body Shop cosmetics. Instead, contemporary brands tend to be more independent of products. A brand like Nike or Mercedes now encompasses a wide range of different effects (cars, bikes, sunglasses, and sportswear). The brand stands for a particular affective relation to a product or an activity. The key to the Nike brand's value is that jogging or merely wearing a shoe feels different if the logo is there. The more this particular effective pattern is repeated across various activities and social situations, the more valuable the Nike brand (presently at $ 9.26 billion).

So the brand is something as weird as a 'propertied effective pattern.' It is a medium that mediates our relations to things, activities, and (often) each other in a particular way. The key to successful brand management is thus to make the brand enter into different forms of communication and interaction and mediated these so that they tend to reproduce the particular effective pattern (the feel, mood, or experience) that stands at the heart of the brand, in such ways that it adds to brand value.

In brand management, the communicative construction of an ethical surplus in the form of a shared social world is put to work to generate surplus value.

But at the same time, this ethical productivity has been much empowered by new information and communications technologies and the breakdown of old traditions and rigid social roles. It is the potential of this empowered and socialized productivity that I would like to work on in the future.

These phenomena do not represent only a market niche because they are the companies and brand's rational responses to a more profound structural change. This deep transformation is made of two main elements. On the one hand, there is the rise of what we call 'the productive publics' and on the other hand the growth of the economy reputation.

In the book, we show how the "productive publics" are becoming increasingly crucial for the organization of both the immaterial and the material. The 'productive publics' identify collaborative networks of strangers who interact in a highly mediatic way (which often doesn't need the use of informatic networks or social media) and coordinates their interactions by sharing a common set of values. By coordinating production in such a way, the productive publics are different from markets and bureaucracies because they allow considering as good reasons a wider range of issues. They tend to be highly independent in conferring a value to the productive contribution of their members. In the book, we suggest that the productive publics are becoming increasingly influential in the information economy, not only in alternative circuits, like Free Software but also within the corporate economy itself, especially around the immaterial assets in some sectors two-thirds of the market value. As a result, a recent growing emphasis on ethics and social responsibility in corporations can be understood to accommodate the orders of worth promoted by the productive public. The other transformation is a consequence of the first one. Companies and brands and knowledge workers are evaluated by other public members to which they belong, based on specific values to which that particular public is devoted. This evaluation leads to a reputation value that can be quantified through direct ratings, e.g., the number of re-tweets, the number of 'likes,' and any other kind of feeling expression.

The brand and company's reputation in the publics determines its ability to attract talent and push it to overcome its duty; engaging non-salaried people (i.e., the productive publics) in co-developing products and services; and to establish a convention of value among consumers that distinguishes the company and its products from its competitors. This is the main driver behind the growing importance of reputation, bringing corporate investments towards CSR and ethical consumerism.

So, yes, CSR, ethical consumerism, corporate values, and so on are an illusion. Still, this illusion has been placed there to manage a much more important trend: the socialization not only of wealth production (as it happens in productive publics) but also the ability to determine the value of that wealth through the economy of reputation. It is this double tendency that we try to capture the core of this book.

Exploitation is a universal phenomenon. We need to find out how it takes place and how wide it is. We believe that an ethical economy harbors the possibility of a new way to reconnect the economy to society and democratize the economy, especially for what concerns the value of attribution and distribution issues. Even if unable to eliminate exploitation itself, this model could lower the system's exploitation level if we compare it to the present neoliberal model. New forms of exploitation are less related to the Marxist idea of 'theft of labour time' and more connected to common resources wealth appropriation, resources that derive from heavily socialized productive networks. An ethical economy based on reputation might become a way to determine, in a more democratic way, who can legitimately claim those resources and in which amount.

ZOE ROMANO: In the introduction of your book, you write: "In a universalist ethical system, the value of one's virtue depends on its ability to contribute to the realization of universal principles of moral conduct. In a system of networked ethics, the value of one's virtue depends on the positive difference made by people who live close to each network." In this way, reputation becomes a useful measure of the productive power that can be translated into non-monetary gratification. Still, it also works as capital used to mobilize resources and start new projects. On the one hand, we are assisting at an abundance of social production. At the same time, we face a new kind of shortage: creating sustainable social relations to start a joint production. Insufficient is the ability to create something together, a koinonia, in a situation of diversity and complexity. Can you list some practical examples of this situation and explain the power games at stake?

ADAM ARVIDSSON: Within management thought, this has been debated for a long time. There is a general recognition that the real key to value is creating a shortage like in a 'culture that leans toward innovation' or a brand that offers a unique experience. The fact that the value shifts from things to enabling people to create cohesion among things is not new. The same principle is applied to the alternative of productive publics, like the Free Software communities. What makes these formative moments to work is not the technical abilities per se, but the ability to create an experience of affective proximity that motivates people to contribute and can identify and attract skilled individuals.

What are the power dynamics at stake? Well, of course, we live in a mediatic system that extremely wealthy actors dominate, so the ability to create ethical capital comes from their market power. However, we think that a new media system is coming, in which power is or could be distributed more equally. The evaluation of that capital happens in ways that allow broader deliberative processes. Yet, this is still a possibility and unnecessary; a lot depends on how media are regulated. For example, will Facebook be able to do data mining on its 500 million users? Should it be possible to exclude other actors from the access of such data? Facebook data, for example, would be an excellent resource to create a system able to obtain a peer-based evaluation of corporate social impact. It is essential to start facing these political issues that concern, for example, how to rethink access to data.

"The ethical problem is intimately linked to the issue of cooperation. It is because people cooperate and create things together that they are ethical beings. Traditionally ethics and economics have been kept apart. Economics has been understood as the realm of objective needs and rational calculus. Simultaneously, the 'softer' ethical problem of how we matter to each other was thought of as something that arose only when one left the workplace and engaged in other forms of social intercourse. However, things like ethical consumerism or corporate ethics indicate that this boundary is no longer as rigid as before.

The introduction of ethics into mainstream economic thought is precisely a response to the new economic centrality of cooperation. Of course, collaboration has always been the secret productive force of capitalism. Both Adam Smith and Karl Marx stressed how industrial production efficiency rested mainly on its ability to create new and more efficient forms of cooperation, like the division of labour in the manufacture, and latter the assembly line and the complex production and distribution systems that developed around it. Marx was particularly foresighted in this respect. In an obscure passage from Grundrisse (a collection of sketches and notebooks that he never intended to publish himself), he argues that as the large-scale industry develops and becomes more complex, the main productive force will be cooperation itself. He called this General Intellect by referring to a sort of social intelligence, a collection of competencies, know-how, and skills that arose organically out of the complex forms of cooperation and social interaction that the large factory-made possible. Machines were an essential part of this General Intellect, but they did not exhaust the concept. Firstly, Marx argued that devices (or technology) resulted from this social intelligence; they were a materialization of knowledge and skills that had already developed through previous forms of cooperation. Secondly, he argued that machines and technology's most important contribution was that they permitted more complex cooperation forms, thus further unleashing the key cooperative or ethical, productive force.

Marx wrote this in the 19th century. When he thought of General Intellect, he thought of the transmission-belts of huge steam-driven factories. But today's Information and Communication Technologies has generalized this enhanced capacity for cooperation across the whole social body. The General Intellect of the factory has become a mass intellectuality that empowers social relations' cooperative potential generally. This is the fundamental element of the new economy. The production of knowledge, experiences, and creativity of all the immaterial goods that Global hope will keep Denmark wealthy is in every case premised on the ability to activate and utilize the productive potential of social cooperation. The cooperation of the many networked multitudes produces an ethical surplus, social relations, experiences, knowledge, and styles that supply the raw material for the new, ethical economy. We would go as far as to say that the information economy's main economic contribution has been that it has enabled these new forms of productive cooperation, this new ethical economy.

That a generalized, technology-enhanced capacity for manifold cooperation has become the main productive force that means no contradiction exists between ethics and economics. On the contrary, the ethical ability to open up to and share with others has become the most fundamental quality of a successful economic agent. This also means that the old models for institutionalizing ethics and economics, representative democracy, and private property are becoming obsolete. Politics is no longer a separate practice, best handled by expert politicians.

Contrary to the primary political method of constructing a familiar social world, an ethical surplus has become a fundamental aspect of economic production. A brand community is like a social movement, open source is a political program, and a self-managed slum or a cooperative micro-credit system is also a project for a different political order. Private property, mainly as applied to immaterial goods like knowledge and innovations, goes against the whole logic of maximizing sharing and cooperation that stands behind the new economy. This means that a successful policy for the new economy cannot just be a matter of surface alterations to an outdated neo-liberal model. The whole institutional order of society needs to be thought through again. It must be geared towards maximizing the cooperative abilities, the ethical production of the many".

"We use the term' ethical economy' not because we think that present productive conditions are necessarily more excellent or more socially conscious, but because the economy of technologically enhanced networks of cooperation puts the ethical dimension of human existence directly to work. This is the sense that the ethics of the particular encounter is a determining factor behind its economic productivity. Value, the value of an actor or a service, becomes primarily based on his or her ability to matter in an ethical sense, give something back, and expand the ethical surplus produced in the encounter. We suggest that the three general principles put forth by Peitersen and Skibsted can be useful to think about the ethical productivity of actors and meetings.

Proximity: Actors are best suited to matter to those things or people to which they feel closeness. This means that actors should be empowered and given maximum freedom to determine their horizons of action. It also means that the management and evaluation of a productive activity should occur as close as possible to where it matters, ideally by the actors present in its proximity-horizon.

Maximization: Each actor's productive potential should be maximized by choosing the actions that generate the most significant added value to his or her proximity-horizon. On a macro level, this means improving sharing instead of competition and encouraging self-organization instead of discipline.

Expansion: An economic agent is more productive the wider his or her horizon of proximity. Thus, it is of economic importance for the agent to continuously expand its closeness feeling: to get involved with more people and situations. Actors should be encouraged to learn from and coach each other; policy should promote the highest degrees of tolerance and respect. Not primarily because these are superior humanistic values, but because, as Richard Florida has so convincingly demonstrated, they are vital economic resources."

The brand is the perfect mechanism to achieve just that.

If you think of it, a brand is a strange kind of object. It is not merely a symbol of a product (that was true up until the 1950s, more or less), nor is it only an extension of a product, an immaterial extra as in Camel cigarettes or the life-style of Camel cigarettes the ethical engagement of Body Shop cosmetics. Instead, contemporary brands tend to be more independent of products. A brand like Nike or Mercedes now encompasses a wide range of different effects (cars, bikes, sunglasses, and sportswear). The brand stands for a particular affective relation to a product or an activity. The key to the Nike brand's value is that jogging or merely wearing a shoe feels different if the logo is there. The more this particular effective pattern is repeated across various activities and social situations, the more valuable the Nike brand (presently at $ 9.26 billion). So the brand is something as weird as a 'propertied effective pattern.' It is a medium that mediates our relations to things, activities, and (often) each other in a particular way. The key to successful brand management is thus to make the brand enter into different forms of communication and interaction and mediated these so that they tend to reproduce the particular effective pattern (the feel, mood, or experience) that stands at the heart of the brand, in such ways that it adds to brand value. In brand management, the communicative construction of an ethical surplus in the form of a familiar social world is put to work to generate surplus value.

But at the same time, this ethical productivity has been much empowered by new information and communications technologies and the breakdown of old traditions and rigid social roles. It is the potential of this empowered and socialized productivity that I would like to work on in the future."

CHAPTER – 7

Green Collar Jobs

Green jobs, according to the Bureau of Labour Statistics, are classified as "jobs in business that produce goods or services that benefit the environment or conserve natural resources" or "jobs in which workers' duties involve making their establishment's production processes more environmentally friendly or use fewer natural resources."

The Bureau of Labour Statistics categorizes Green Jobs as water conservation, Sustainable forestry, Biofuels, Geothermal energy, environmental remediation, Sustainability, Energy auditors, Recycling, Electric Vehicles, Solar power, and Wind energy.

These definitions include jobs that seek to use or develop renewable forms of energy (i.e., wind, hydropower, geothermal, wind, landfill gas, and municipal solid waste) and increase their efficiency. Under the green jobs domain, education, training, and public awareness are also included. These jobs seek to enforce regulations, support education and increase general influence to benefit the environment. Under the transition from dirty jobs to green jobs, the international labour community has focused on a just transition to ensure that as carbon-intensive jobs disappear, the communities most effect will have opportunities in these other industries.

Agricultural Scientist

Specialize in agricultural productivity. They study commercial plants, animals, and cultivation techniques to improve farms and farming industries' productivity and sustainability. Agricultural scientists have a higher-than-average proportion of full-time jobs, and earnings are above average.

Climate Change Scientist

Research and present data on the structure and dynamics of our climate system. Currently, there is scientific consensus from several American Scientific Societies that the earth's temperature is warming.

Conservation Officer

Advance and ensure the protection of the natural environment and resources via educating communities and encouraging involvement and awareness. The growth of these jobs, along with Forester jobs in the U.S., is predicted to be around 6 percent (in line with average occupation growth) from 2016 to 2026

Ecologist

Investigate ecosystems as a whole, i.e.; they investigate both the living and non-living components of the environment.

They study the various animals and plants that live within an ecosystem and the relationship between them.

Electric Car Engineer

Use science and maths to design and develop electric automobile technology. They then undertake evaluations concerning measuring the designs above' safety, efficiency, cost, reliability, and security. An Electric Car Engineer is just one of a number of possible jobs in the electric vehicle industry. This type of Engineer will work in teams with other kinds of Engineers to produce electric automobiles.

Environmental Engineer

Examine and mitigate the effects of human and other activities on both the natural and built environment. This could include reducing pollution and protecting the air, water, soil, and humans from actions that may harm either them or the environment. According to CNBC, in 2018, this was one of the fastest-growing environmental jobs across the world. The University of Portland recently reported that they would add a clean energy technology minor to enable their environmental engineering graduates to' compete in an expanding ecological job market.'

Environmental Scientist

They examine the environment (for example, by sampling the land, water, air, or other natural resources) and develop policies and plans designed to prevent, control, or reduce the harmful effects of human activity on the environment and also one of the fastest-growing environmental jobs in the world in 2018 according to CNBC.

Environmental Consultant

Analyse and provide advice on policies and processes that guide the design, implementation, and modification of commercial or government environmental operations and programs. Environmental Consultants are often employed to ensure ecological legislation is being adhered to during construction projects. They are listed as one of the top ten fastest-growing green jobs in Australia in 2018.

Environmental Health Officer

Measure risk and develop, oversee, implement and monitor legislation that governs public health for both the built and natural environment. Environmental Health Officers carry out these aforementioned duties to promote good human health and best practices environmentally and. Also one of the fastest-growing environmental jobs in Australia in 2018.

Environmental Manager

Supervise the environmental performance of private companies and public institutions. They also formulate, execute and oversee environmental strategies that encourage sustainable development. A single company can employ an Environmental Manager to ensure any adverse environmental impacts caused by their operation are minimized.

Forestry Manager

In a nutshell, they are responsible for the cultivation of forests. Map out and lead the planting, growth, harvesting, and conservation of forests for wood production. To ensure balance and sustainable development, Foresters may become involved in multipurpose forests, sustainable forest management, and the reforestation of native woodlands. The growth of these jobs, along with Conservation Officer jobs in the U.S., is predicted to be around 6 percent (in line with average occupation growth) from 2016 to 2026

According to the Food and Agriculture Organization of the United Nations, forests provide more than 86 million green jobs and support many more people's livelihoods. An estimated 880 million people worldwide spend part of their time collecting fuelwood or producing charcoal, many of them women. Human populations tend to be low in low-income countries with high forest cover and tall forest biodiversity, but poverty rates in these areas tend to be high. Some 252 million people living in forests and savannahs have incomes of less than USD 1.25 per day.

Green Building Designers

Design buildings (they can be homes, offices, schools, hospitals, or any other type of building) that, in their design, construction or operation, reduce or eliminate adverse impacts and can create positive effects on our climate and natural environment. They also try to reduce negative environmental impacts in terms of reducing the contributions to landfills.

Marine Biologist

Analyse the interplay of marine life (animals and plants) with coastal areas and the atmosphere. And Crucial today is their role in measuring the impact of climate change on our oceans and how much ocean acidification is present and potentially damaging our coral reef ecosystems.

Recycling Worker

In a typical recycling plant (MRF), the workers are sort laborers, equipment operators, managers (various levels), and maintenance mechanics. Also included are drivers who collect the recycled from residential, commercial, and non-hazardous industrial sources. Sort laborers' clean' the stream at various stages of the mechanized sortation process to prevent equipment stoppages and produce bales acceptable to the remanufacturing sector depending on the commodity (metal, paper, cardboard, plastics, etc.).

Equipment operators operate heavy equipment designed to help with processes around the plant. Typical gear includes skid-steers (For cleaning up and moving large amounts of material to bale), forklifts (to move bales and containers of material to places within the plant collected from the sortation process).

Managers typically manage the operations/sales and human resources of the MRF, so the sortation process requiring sorters and equipment operators runs properly day today. Maintenance mechanics work to ensure all equipment works appropriately (such as unjamming a conveyor or fixing electronic equipment associated with the sortation process).

Renewable Energy Engineer

Study how to best supply energy from renewable or sustainable energy sources, such as wind energy, solar power, wave energy, and biofuels. They focus on ways of producing energy that is deemed to be safer for the environment. An Energy Engineer was listed as one of the fastest-growing jobs in Australia in 2018.

Solar Photovoltaic (P.v.) Installers

Assemble and carry out solar panels installation on rooftops or other areas such as ground-mounted solar panels. A growing industry, for example, has seen job creation and on-the-job training by a non-profit called GRID Alternatives.

Urban Farmer

Responsible for growing food in a city or heavily populated town. Green rooftops can provide locally sourced foods that help protect the environment by reducing pesticides, fossil fuels, and other resources that are often used to grow and transport food to market from larger commercial farms.

Water Quality Scientist

Ensure that minimum water quality standards are met and ensure human safety and minimize harm to the natural environment. Water quality scientists ensure that these global standards and other compliance requirements are met in three areas - groundwater, surface water (lakes, rivers, ponds, etc.), and drinking water. "The fact that water is the lifeblood of our planet means that there are thousands of opportunities for environmental workers in this area".

Wind Energy Technician

Wind technicians install, inspect, maintain, operate, and repair wind turbines. Wind technicians have the knowledge to identify and fix issues that could cause the turbine to be break or fail to perform as it should. Globally one of the fastest-growing environmental jobs in 2017. The U.S. Department of Energy is working with six leading wind turbine manufacturers towards achieving 20% wind power in the United States by 2030. However, the dropping number of students in power engineering programs in recent years means that the labour requirements needed to facilitate this aim won't be met unless this trend is reversed.

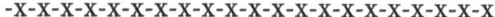

www.ingramcontent.com/pod-product-compliance
Lightning Source LLC
Chambersburg PA
CBHW030906180526
45163CB00004B/1722